THE LADDER

Also by Alan Michael Parker

THE LADDER

ALAN
MICHAEL
PARKER

Tupelo Press
North Adams, Massachusetts

Library of Congress Cataloging-in-Publication Data available upon request.
ISBN: 978-1-936797-74-5

Cover and text designed by Josef Beery
Cover: iStock Photo

First paperback edition: August 2016.

Tupelo Press
P.O. Box 1767, North Adams, Massachusetts 01247
Telephone: (413) 664–9611 / editor@tupelopress.org / www.tupelopress.org

Tupelo Press is an award-winning independent literary press that publishes
fine fiction, nonfiction, and poetry in books that are a joy to hold as well as
read. Tupelo Press is a registered 501(c)(3) nonprofit organization, and we
rely on public support to carry out our mission of publishing extraordinary
work that may be outside the realm of the large commercial publishers.
Financial donations are welcome and are tax deductible.

ART WORKS.
arts.gov

Produced with support from
the National Endowment for the Arts

for Felicia

Contents

The Raking

I want to live in a pyramid of leaves

a red leaf like a gulp of wine
sex   the leaves everywhere

twirl a stem and see
what's turned away from God

pile the leaves again
win one war

a leaf isn't much
I'm not much
a leaf's enough

when the wind spirals
a spout of leaves to air
I want to—

what?   what shall I?

listen   a leaf crushed   a dry star
crumbled in a fist

this life the next life   the crackle

Che cosa faccio? Scrivo.
E come vivo? Vivo.

What do I do? I write.
And how do I live? I live.

—Puccini, *La Bohème*

THE LADDER

I'm Here to Give a Little Talk on Singing

I'm not a man who sings in the shower,

or while mopping the floor
to the rhythm of the mop,
to the muscle and the math,

or when kneading sweet, gluey dough
deeply with my palms and my wrists,
for the best butter cookies,

or when wiping engine oil,
a brushstroke across my forehead,

or bouncing along on the subway
to the museum.
I'm going to the museum,

I'm at the museum
and there's the Chagall —

no matter that my whole body
standing before the Chagall
is the sail of every boat, ever, in every wind.

I'll sing later, after.
I'll sing with the other curmudgeons,
which I am, philosophically—

there's so much to doubt,
and I'm doubt's little monkey.

To sing would be
religious, or sacrilegious;
too soon, I say, too much a promise.

Later, if something or someone
might save me,
or if love lasts,

I'd consider a little singing, maybe.

The Canada Geese

Why does a goose honk when a goose flies?

To understand, I need to fly,
to communicate more politely

with the tops of the trees and their tentative leaves,

and say thank you to the telephone poles
for keeping the fields battened down,

and to the roofs of the barns

like the covers of books
someone fell asleep reading,

and to the town below like a television left on,
thank you for dreaming.

Flying is more like being flown, I think,
the air doing the work.

That's what I would say:
take me,
take care,
care for me,
air.

Enough

I owned a watch
that never kept time,
even when new,

but I wore it anyway
(it was a gift),

and so I had to wear another watch
to keep time,

and I wore a third watch
because it was beautiful

and beauty makes sense.

How many watches?
I covered my arms and legs.
I wore time in bangles and Velcro and leather.
Time was my hat.

I was a tree with all my rings everywhere,
and a planet strapped into orbit.

I showed everyone all my ideas,
my thunderous, ticking heart.

Like anger and love I wound myself automatically.
Like history my faces glowed.
Like sadness I circled myself.

When time is enough
I shall stop.
I will lay me down on a grassy bed by a stream
that moves by
(and moves by).

A Partial List of Our Demands

Lord, let us not kill one another.
Except for the infidels.
And the irritating people.
And the people who refuse to be compassionate,
especially when driving.
Lord, let us choose:
Isn't free will ours?
On that matter, you could answer.

Lord, we know enough
to collect shiny things
and stash them in our nests,
and to eat everything on our plates
in case there's no food tomorrow
or someone wants what we have.
But Lord, you've left us despairing

of due process, and a secure server,
and an injury-free season
(admittedly, that's a personal comment),
and a little natural beauty
not so far away.
Of course, you could just
send a note, Lord, or a bird.
There's no need to insist we believe.

It's okay, Lord.
It must be so hard to be you
and feel under the weather.
Soon you'll be yourself again.
Perhaps you'll meet our children,
or their children, or their children's children:
children can be fun
when they're not all yours.
But you know that already, Lord.

Maybe there will be a little party
and some fireworks;
fireworks are such wonderful
imitations of you.
There could be a long line of dancing—
don't worry, not a conga,
this isn't a cruise ship—
and a sing-along, and a piñata.
Although it might be wise for you
to work on your public speaking, Lord.
As is, allowing our failures
to stand for your love
isn't really success.

Let us know when you're ready
to hazard a new approach:
we'll be here, Lord, practicing.

Pushing Back

The memory of a man comes back—

He was on his cell phone, calling someone back,
Walking around a corner onto 7th Avenue,
You could hear him shouting,

And the wind held him back,
And he put out his hands
Into the careless weather,

Pushing forward, pushing back,
Saying stop, no, as his tie flapped over a shoulder
And his trench coat billowed,

And you were a boy, looking back,
And he was flying, he was dead,
For the first time you thought of death,

For he could go no further, nor go back.
You see him now, years later,
With your sympathy, and seeing him

Is a kind of love. Every memory pushes back,
A continuing, keeping us,
A stay.

Saying stop, no, not today, pushing back.

The Dog Misses You

The dog went out to look for you. She wore a big blue ribbon, in case of a situation. She circumnavigated the yard. She has been practicing saying *I love you* in every language. *Aku sampeyan*, the dog practices saying in Javanese. *Te iubesc*, the dog practices saying in Romanian. She has also been practicing saying *I'm lost* in every language. *Kur kev prob lawm*, the dog practices saying in Hmong. *Jien mitlufa*, the dog practices saying in Maltese.

The dog dug a hole along the fence. She's so funny when she digs, all that dirt flying. There is surely a different world on the other side of the fence. The fence could be Time: on this side, the years are kept. Are you over there?

In the afternoon, the dog pulled the leash so hard, she lifted off, above the trees. You weren't to be found, but there were some remarkable children waiting. Later that night, in the tidy evening, the dog put her blocky head upon the kitchen floor, listening and sleeping, one soft and floppy ear pressed into the future. There she wondered about the sadnesses that only she could sense.

Góður hundur, the dog practices saying in Icelandic. *Maayo nga iro*, the dog practices saying in Cebuano. *Bon chien*, the dog practices saying in French. Good dog, good dog, good dog. And then the dog practices saying in Esperanto *I'm lost, mi perdis*.

The dog has three wishes left. She wishes she knew where to find you. She wishes you would come home with a treat. She wishes you and I were together on the bed, and up she would jump.

The Ladder

When I finally made my way across the ice
of my twenties and thirties and forties

and up the mountain through the cedars,
a great sage gave me a grass sack

to start my new life.
In the grass sack I found

a dull gray stone,
a box that once held a gold locket,

a toy fire truck, and a ladder.
I have learned to use the stone

in love, to turn the stone over.
I keep the box closed,

the gift its own cherishing.
The toy fire truck—well,

fate burns, as it will.
The great sage said a grass sack

is a thing, just a thing,
all things empty.

But Master, the ladder.
I hitched up the ladder to every height,

and still the moon rolls away.
Above the clouds

the airplanes are small and cold,
and the ladder sways.

Teach me to climb
down from ambition.

Beyond my fingertips
rolls the moon.

On Not Burning a Matisse

If I could pick one work by Matisse
to steal
and not set on fire

and let my attorney tell the judge
He wouldn't have set that Matisse on fire

I would probably choose his relatively unknown print
"The Nightmare of the White Elephant"

before which I would dress up
like an elephant
and troika and curtsy and do backflips

and I'd hide the Matisse
in the left atrium of my heart
every time my brother the lawyer
an officer of the court
comes to town to play basketball

because I want the work of art
to fill my feelings
with an elephant's loneliness

and wrack my nights with my own insufficiency
and remind me of my guilt

because even when stolen
any hope is hope

The Use of the Second Person

You were never alone: we are all here too.
You, who were always a boy in a brutal hat,
head down over his geometry
and a slice in a back booth at Frank's,

were never all of the boys,
never a symbol running away from its thing.

Maybe there wasn't a baseball bat
swung at your life, and life
wasn't a baseball bat swung at you,
but you ditched anyway.
From the doctor's waiting room,
someone's grandmother inside,
from the Spanish teacher, *no se,*
from the new Thanksgiving war movie,
even from what wasn't swung at you,
you tore away.

We see you, sing the prices of the stuff.
Welcome home, winks the keyhole.
Wanna, says the psycho in the sex boots.
Feel that, says the sun, finally going down.

You are beyond gesture, and still a beckoning.
You are the wrong word in the wrong mouth,
maybe in my mouth, maybe this word is wrong.
You are tomorrow too soon, oh god.
But someone is calling. That's your phone
chirping and tingling in a back pocket.
Your phone has been trying you all day,
your phone wants to listen to you,
your phone loves you,
answer your phone.

Warm Night, Stay

Warm night, stay.
The bed, the room, the block, the city,
the taxis cutting to.
The outside pours away
between your fingers
as they twitch, resting on my chest,
the prow of the dream.
Warm night, stay.

Warm night, stay.
A strand of hair dreams a river.
Your nightgown twists, your hip tight,
and you scratch above your breast,
half a scratch, half a moon.

Warm night, stay. The leaves
of the ficus by the window
rustle, one side real.
That's what a dreamer is,
one side real.

Warm night, stay.
The sheet and blanket pile,
sloughed upon a mountain dreamed.
The sheet and blanket pile
in a cloud
clapped by a dreamer.
The sheet and blanket pile,
galloped by a dreamer.

Warm night, stay.
Your right leg rolls
upon me, how a dream
rolls and settles, weighs.
If I move, you move.

Love, stay.
Propped on the deck on the ship
of the warm night, dreaming,
rocked by the steady steamer of your breathing,
wherever you are going,
warm night, stay.

The Cossacks

My great-grandmother was never wrong
the way old people are never wrong.
Every morning I went to her apartment—
maybe I was four?—

like a peddler in one of her stories
who walks miles between two villages
selling potatoes and walking back
and buying a chicken and walking back

and the meanest horse of a Cossack
hears the peddler trudge on
and kicks the stall door

and the sunset is pretty
but no one can eat pretty.

If there had been a dragon
or a rocket
or a river
or even a girl in the story—

but my great-grandmother
had lived too long for such nonsense.

When the Cossacks stormed our game
she and I lay down and hid in the ditch
behind the couch in the living room

terrified by the high-stepping hooves of the horses.

My Hair

Not to be vainglorious,
but I've just grown my hair again—
doesn't it look fabulous!

When the weeds came, I let them.
When a deer came, I ate it.
When the jungle came, I roared.

No one knew me anymore
because of my new hair
(when have I been shaggy and lustrous),
so I was safe:

I could finally write an illegal poem to the government,

and a poem that tells all of your secrets,

and a poem that forgets its lines,

and an almost beautiful poem,

and a poem that feeds the hungry,

and an unbearable poem.

I am hidden by my hair.
It's mythical, my hair.

Now, when the tree on the mountain
sees my hair
and shivers and sways
in envy,
I will know what to say:

I am so sorry, tree,
you must be very cold.
Try being less scared
of dying.

Another Bug

For a man to be undone
by a bug
can screw up
his sense of justice.

To get to this porch,
the bug somehow survived
being dipped in paint,
its forelegs or antennae or feelers

or whatever those are
slapped with latex, off-white.

The man can picture
the bug stuck to the living-room wall
then squirming free.

Now the bug arrives
upon the man's flip-flop
and scampers further up
to survey the world from his right knee.

It was the brilliant Hilde Meiner who wrote,
"Individualism is humanity's great melodrama."

One painted foreleg
twitches and waves, the flag of
a Greek philosopher surrendering.

To freak out the man.
If only he didn't identify.
All that universal suffering.

After Love

I wrote letters of introduction
and sent them to every embassy
of every future
just in case you need something
when you get there

including to all the outposts of wind-up afternoons
and to all the banquets where the gods disagree
and to all the bees muscling in all the flowers
and of course to every color.

In the letters I share a couple of our secrets
the story of our argument on the way to Toronto
how we drove by Toronto arguing
because you were wrong

and later the sweet closing of your body
on my Niagara Falls my Maid of the Mist
and how in love
you breathe in as though you were laughing.

Your right hand rubs my scalp
scratching without thinking
after love
as though my head were your own.
I put that in a few of the letters.
I hope this is all okay.

Now wherever you go they'll know you
and you'll be asked to accompany
all of the presidents
every grain of blue

and all of the ministers
every knife of every poplar
and all of the other world's ambassadors
every cogitating groundhog.
I wouldn't mind being there
to see.

Though my first obligation is right here
as you rise after love
to dress back-lighted and so slowly

as each gesture rounds off
how the light feels about the room.

Everyone should know.
I will write more letters.

The Serengeti

On her way home she rose from the close crowd in the subway
into the summer air like a hot plum fleshy and wet
and turned right to turn right into her regular bodega
for a six-pack a salad a cheap DVD a bottle of seltzer
but her soul turned left

She saw the blades of the air slowly spin
a nanny a stroller a cop three gossipy clutches of uniformed girls
as her soul waited at the light and crossed away into some blueness
as though the city were a Serengeti and her soul
thirsty no water no relief
but slowly like a small storm moving on too

She had been to the Serengeti once as a child with her aunt
but why the Serengeti the blueness and the brown
falling through another brown like time itself

She came out to hold her plastic bag of groceries and look
at her soul standing over there
and she wondered about her date to come tonight
the chatty nurse a little younger and how his soul might be in scrubs
elsewhere on the Serengeti on the Serengeti
you could live and never meet on the Serengeti of your very own

Like news disappearing today nearby the rush-hour traffic went
the other traffic across the median like news tomorrow
radios doors locked inside thoughts with hopes
but her soul turned downtown but her apartment was uptown
how long could a person live like this walking apart on the Serengeti
where did her soul go

The Sweetness of the Nectarine

The bent-over old guy
trudging up
a rocky hill
while munching a juicy nectarine
feels okay, not great.
His watch is broken.
Twice a day, he stops
dying.
He thinks, I should
never have snapped
all that anger
over my knee.

Postcard from Spain

Thanks for your card. I like hearing from you.
What a great picture, too: there must be
a million people on that beach in Barcelona,
so many outfits and towels and umbrellas.
And your note is wry:
"The cyber café has the cheapest postcards."
It's different these days, even somewhat eerie
that a postcard can be from a life
lived two weeks ago—now that the Internet
has made the past and present one.
And Instagram and Tumblr together
are like the Big Bang:
you're everywhere at once in Spain,
with a toothache at the pharmacy,
sipping an icy lemonade in a park
then dipping your bandana in the fountain,
finding the darkness in you
is Goya's. But I'm so glad you wrote
and thought to share: thank you.
Yes, I'm mostly recovered, the family's well—
though no one understands Aunt Martha anymore,
which has an upside,
you know what Aunt Martha can be like.
I appreciate your thoughtfulness.
Thanks to you, I see again
the face of the clerk at the post office
in the tenderness of her hijab,
how perfectly her sigh made her lips purse
when she smiled at my awful Spanish
and counted out my change
slowly in impeccable English,
as though I were no smarter
than her stapler. But she liked me,

I could tell: our moment was shared,
irrespective of her politics or mine.
I have been thinking a lot about the light
I glimpsed in her kind irony,
as though I could see
the unflickering living candle of her.
She liked that I was mailing myself a postcard.

A Poppy Seed

I was on the phone and trying to buy concert tickets,

but I was distracted by a poppy seed,
yes, a poppy seed, a single one,

the round and hard taste of it,
the way it's so clearly
never a blueberry between my teeth,

there's nothing to explode inside a poppy seed,
no memories, it's like an answer,
it's so small in light of everything,

but still I try to remind myself,
there are molecules and atoms:
a poppy seed is huge.

The woman on the phone was saying,
Sir? Sir? Are you ready? Sir?
Sir, do you have your information, Sir?

but I wasn't ready,
I didn't have my information,
I had nothing right,

because I wanted to listen to the poppy seed,
if only we could talk together
like childhood friends, this little asteroid and I,

and then the conversation would turn,
as it does,
around the curve of the Earth

to the possible wholeness, for example, of God.

Let's Go: Arkansas

We'll bring the money from the sock drawer, the money in the sock, we'll take the sock to the bus station to count the money, we'll buy the bus tickets, some of us like to wait outside, to go to Arkansas.

Everyone's a novel, the bus will fill with novels, who can read them all, the seats will feel like something forgotten from childhood until now, and the tinted windows will be like looking through a bug's eyes, or a low-level angel's eyes, or the eyes of a sleepy dog, or from inside a glass of water.

The world will be continuous until Arkansas. We'll know that the world is continuous when the bus stops and we're not there yet. It's like how we know we're alive, like that moment yesterday, buying a new phone for the trip to Arkansas, hand to heart, what's that weird giddyup in my chest, what's this new bass line?

We'll eat food from its wrappers dropped inside machines, pulled from machines, because that's what the food is for, because we are like this food in the world, our thoughts and our bodies, like food coming out of the wrapper a bit.

Arkansas must be here. Maybe we'll be in Arkansas by Father's Day and all the new fathers in Arkansas will sit at their tables and open cards from their kids who can't read or write yet, from their babies, because that's what we're like in our lives, we're like babies in the universe, in relation to knowledge, we're like babies but we're learning, and now we're in Arkansas, we're here, everybody off. Arkansas, last stop.

The Artist and His Model

Holding up a fish and lecturing,
maybe on the quality of the catch,
my friend, a three-inch Chinese figurine,

lolls on my desk,
clay legs splayed,
clay pants and clay shirt.

Of course, I mostly also
sit around and pontificate,
expound when no one's here.

And I've been formed.
And I've been haggled into being,
shaped by a consciousness

I can't know,
in which I don't believe.

And I'm a tourist's solace.
And I'm a gift from my wife.
And I don't want to leave my room.

We're so tiny in the world:
if only he could speak and I could listen,

then all of the other inanimate objects
might have souls, and my
metaphysical paranoia could be confirmed,

and my shame would be deserved,
for how I treat things.
Shame is so rarely deserved.

He looks to be about seventy,
and I look like a Jewish Sir Ben Kingsley
when I fantasize that I've been knighted.

When I fantasize that I've been
reincarnated, that's different, then I know
to expect less.

Just today, the man on my desk
was declaiming, the way he does forever,
clay man, clay fish,

and I had nothing,
and so I made myself
a tuna sandwich in his honor,

and we sat together and listened
to the latest wars on the radio.

The Canada Geese

What does the goose think I'm doing?
I wave. I might as well

be a sunflower, one-legged, done.
Maybe I'm a manhole, all face.
Or maybe I'm the tiniest pond.

Maybe I'm always
a sad emergency,
running outside to see, to see.

Reading *Antony and Cleopatra* at the Airport Again

On the ground by gate 17, concourse B,
the giant planes do-si-do, delayed,
cockpits lighted,
as the sky rolls out above the runways,
and a herd of clouds
parades off-stage to the south
like the elephants of another country's history.

It's too late on a Sunday night
for travelers all to take the world
personally, faces tight,
pacing and eating, tucking in
the kids by phone, being here, not home.

Working at a kiosk, a bored teen with a nose ring
worries a lock of her hennaed hair
as she sells a huge green mug
to a Packers fan bedecked in green,
while his huge green friends nearby
belly themselves up to beers at the bar.

But now she's reading again
her thumbed copy of *Antony and Cleopatra*:
maybe there will be a test in the morning,
where's the battle, who's the general,
who's a friend, where's the lover.

Or maybe she imagines her real lover
deployed with the Army Rangers in Pakistan.
I only have a partial view, it's all we ever get,

despite how great the windows are,
how theatrical the curve of the earth,
the arms of the beloved, the lighted sky
minus the moon. The moon would,
of course, finish the scene, signify.

I want her boyfriend to text
that her barge is ready, the sails
trimmed for life together upon any Nile,
let's go, who cares who knows
we never passed History,
our love besieged by the armies of money.

I am dying, Egypt, dying.
Give me some wine and let me speak a little.
When she lays the book aside
to help another customer,
a bracelet snakes down her wrist.

I'm another customer: I buy
a bottle of water and a pack of gum I'll never chew
just to get a glimpse up close
of her movie-star eyeliner.

Ein Künstlerroman

When I was young, I lived for a summer

in an apartment with five other graduate students in a city called
Here We Go,

and we had no shower, no dishwasher, no modesty, no willpower,
no iron, no mop, no broom, no elevator, no view, no beckoning
rooftop, no rigorous thinking, poor sense,

but we did have hot water at 2 p.m. for half an hour, and certitude,
and a cat named Joseph Cornell,

and bad booze, and some sex, and still not as much as everyone
else seemed to be having,

and we had a dryer and a refrigerator standing next to one another
in a room that our landlord called a kitchen.

We got high on myth: we were the myth.

We put the milk in the dryer and made a carton of cartoon clouds.

We put Rebecca's wet green sweater in the freezer, and the next
day the sweater looked like a land mass, a vast tundra with two
peninsulas upon which caribou might gather. Or reindeer—who
could guess what snorted and munched in that frozen room all
night, so dreamed.

And I read Heidegger, and I was made new.

That was the summer that hell was as hot as a dryer in hell.

What could we know? Our exuberance compensated for our panic, and our fussiness was prophetic; and we were acolytes, apprenticed to indifference and appearance; and our lives were designed for use, for the machines that made memories of music; and we only vaguely noted the associative properties of capital; and we lived with books as icons, with services and without goods; and our doubt resounded in the hollows of our style; and we believed in ideas as currency.

That was the summer I met me.

I put my soul in the dryer, and out came a poem.

I put my poem in the refrigerator, and out came a life.

River Birches

I would leave for a better place—
        not death, not *a better place*, not that wish—
but somewhere by a stone wall and a stand of river birches,
the trees peeling and papery in winter.
        Yes, I am a fool to love
                some trees that don't exist
instead of being here. I know.
Still the river birches
        and the haphazard ruin of the stone wall
together make a thought
I feel.
            No one lives there yet,
there is no hate,
and that is where I'd go.

The Last Page

I have stopped reading the last page of novels—
now the horse drags the rider down the lane

and through the sugarcane field
to the impossibly brown sea

and that's where they stop, just short.
Now the sun turns to look.

I have stopped believing what's next:
I have laid down my knitting of time.

I have left the pillowcase off
of the perfect afternoon.

As for the final square of chocolate,
lie there uneaten, my shiny, silver joy.

I have stopped smoking every cigarette.
I have stopped cutting the cut grass.

Oh, little bird, abide with me
before the stars go out,

before the handle turns,
before the floorboards creak awake,

before anyone rises to a bell.
Pertaining to the spirit, I can only suggest

try a cool washcloth for the heat.
I have driven off without my change,

stopped one block shy
of the last block on earth.

Mom, go back to your hospital room, your lilac
nightgown still on your small shoulders.

Letter to the Grand High Commissioner
of the Maltese Police Marching Band

Dear Sir or Madam:

I write to express my admiration for your flag. It's so warmly blue,
it redefines patriotism. You have the best flag waving on any island,
a flag grand enough to wrap a capital city and still have room for
the hospital on the hill. I can picture those attending nuns with
their peekaboo nun toes.

But I have concerns about the music. Have you considered that
since your fine band plays in such narrow streets, the stone
buildings bounce the sounds sideways, against the walls, and as
a result the front of the band and the back of the band can't hear
the other play? The song's so out of sync, it's like the ending and
the beginning play at once, or the ending doesn't remember the
beginning. And the poor middle! The middle is always either
ahead or behind, and sometimes first, and other times last. It's
confusing, dear Sir or Madam.

I suspect the source of the problem may be time. Here's an analogy.
Think of how religions continue to commit to fundamental
principles no longer relevant, precepts scientifically disproved.
Here's another analogy, maybe a better one, considering the
martial manner of your repertoire; think of how a war is always
bloodier than anyone predicts.

Permit me a suggestion: disarm your officers. Tell the brass to
finger their horns and only pretend to blow. Tell the drum line
to pantomime. Tell the xylophone no. Tell the piccolos to piccolo
as though. Tell the band to march and smile and wave their
instruments—since it's apparent that you must parade each night,
all along Triq ir-Reppublika. You're a police band, I understand,
and you must serve the rule of law symbolically, but please.

Respectfully, as ever, yours—

Letter to the Buddha, Including an X-ray of My Foot

So now you know even more
than everything, now you see
how unfinished I am
in the rooms
of my body.

There went Sue the X-ray technician
running to hide in the lead booth
like the Bodhisattva of Fear Itself.
And here is the body in black-and-white,
moonlight on a playground:

the twenty-six bones of the foot:
talus, calcaneus, cuniforms I, II & III,
cuboid and navicular. Five metatarsals,
two phalanges in the great toe,
three phalanges in the other four.

What does an X-ray X-ray?
The forty-two muscles,
the thirty-two joints, the more than
fifty ligaments and tendons, and the more than
250,000 sweat glands of the foot

seen through—as the Unknown
thumps shut the door to the X-ray booth,
the sound on the intercom
the sound of Sue whistling.
Hold still. Don't breathe. Good.

Master, I'm sending you a picture of my foot,
the one that hurts,
a foot made in the world, pain
you could teach me not to need.
There. Good. Done.

I am writing to say that I'm sorry
there's still stuff I want,
that the hospital smell of the chemicals
feels like it burns, that I hope
no human foot hurts again.

Yes, we both know that I'm not better.
But I am writing to say that it's okay,
that you can let go of worrying about me.
Buddha, they took an X-ray.
Buddha, the X-ray was negative.

Fetch

Oh, to be the happy dog
trotting back.

The dog's named Please
as she waits,

Thank You as she goes.
The sky helps, too.

Really, love,
I just want

to bring to you the moon
dripping in my jaws.

The Widow

I.
Instead of returning to the apartment
after the funeral
she balls her veil into her clutch

and begs a cigarette
from one of the boys
always hanging around the freight door.

It's too hot to smoke, but the boy's
pretty, hand up and dangling from
the heavy door's strap.

Years ago, when she was still playing
at being older, she found
in a vintage store downtown

an antique, cocktail-length cigarette holder,
one thin crack in the bone
where someone's teeth had come down hard.

Somehow, every symptom
becomes its disease,
even playing old, she thinks,

even memory.
The boys outside the freight door
are respectful, smiling, nodding,

scared of her, together
sucking in each solid breath.
She speaks no Spanish.

2.
Life's a beaded dress
she should have bought.

Life is only
as good
as the water is cold
on the hottest day.

Life is that funny novel
she once read.

Life throws a child up into
the air
and catches her,
a woman.

3.
The problem with starting smoking again
is that she sees her hands,

the veins' insistence,
the mined blue that settles.

Two knuckles kink with arthritis,
the joints grown over.

Here, she thought to try a little ruination,
and there, it's already done.

She pockets the boy's lighter,
for a little while.

Candying Mint

Strip thirty good-sized leaves.
Wash them, and pat dry.

Paint the leaves with egg white
and dredge in fine sugar.
Let stand upon a wire rack.

Buber writes, "Man's final objective is this:
to become, himself, a law—a Torah."

The granules glimmer upon the mint,
hard dew, a glittery,
sweet finish to a fine night

and a flourless chocolate cake
with a little raspberry sauce.

I know that it's my job, but Rabbi, I worry
because I like worrying,
and I admire the persistence of the mint,

really just a weed: spicy, ragged, alive.
To grow toward the sun—it's like listening—

and who doesn't need to aspire?
Yes, Rabbi, the lesson's true:
to become a law means to know God,

but who could be ready for that?
Rabbi, try the candied mint: it's heaven.

A Late September Afternoon in the Office of the Birches

Sometimes, a squirrel like a thought
agitates through the leaves.
Scrabbling up the bark curls
of a birch tree, almost free.

When I close my eyes,
the cool moss on the rock
against my cheek feels like a memory
I can't recall—ice cream? peaches?

Sometimes, the wind delivers.
But there are no messages.
In a boulder in the clearing
a gash of blue quartz pulses, fixed.

One characteristic of light: it reaches.
Sometimes, the wind sloughs into readiness,
silent upon the strings of the birches,
and like the deer I raise my head.

Influenza Ode (From a Very Tall Building)

From here, the farthest highway
        slammed with cars
arrives to the eye in segments
        slicing through the baffling clouds,
shiny as the bite of a memory
        of being yelled at, a call to the kitchen
for a late-night admonition,
        while the dirty river to the harbor
dries like mustard upon the evening meat.
        The worser I feel, the childer I am.
Beyond the window, I can see
        how the moody wind manipulates,
the splat of springtime
        muddled in some illegible smatter,
while the rooftops pretend to organize—
        a scripture of rooftops,
dishes and antennae—and jumbled,
        over-heated gardens snarl in disuse.
From this far away the occasional bird
        blackens in silhouette, little rabbi.
From this far away a rabbinate of birds
        swoops above the alleys below,
a gulp of swallows.
        The trees evangelize the season,
the light clear as sick soup.
        The sky's a laryngitis.
Shiver me in your arms, my fever—
        my life untied, a hospital gown.

Roadkill

When I find you, darling, in the night
curled on the rug in the living room,
insomniacal as the TV—
though the dog's happy, the coffee cake's happy,

the chamomile tea's happy—
and you're crying, and I ask what happened,
and you answer "roadkill,"
for a moment I'm sure you mean that's

what we are in the universe,
because that's how each day makes us feel.
A clump of hair in a drain, pickings,
the darkness rubbing us away.

With my hand like a small paw,
I hesitate, then touch your shoulder.

A Poem for Sally

He thought he might swallow whole
his youngest daughter, if she didn't stop
hurting herself. She would complain,

of course, carry on inside his big dad-belly,
but she would be safe there
until she was ready to come back.

He would swallow the moon
to keep her company, one white slice
sliding down to arrive in her arms,

and he would drink and drink a river
so she could see how beautiful.
Things would be comforting—stuff to touch—

but she would probably need something to do.
Maybe he would swallow for her
a rowboat with a trolling motor,

and maybe a jug of O.J.,
and maybe even an mp3 player.
Ashore, she could ride her own small horse

if she wanted. She could eat cheesecake,
wear the bangled green skirt,
sing badly, softly, always shy,

no need for pain.
Peace, the fish dreamy, all music,
as the cranes or egrets—

some kind of giant bird—would unfold
awkwardly their paperclip bodies,
flap in slo-mo their wings,

and then launch themselves
wide and low over the marsh grass.
The stars would burn into the sky behind her,

and she would row into the middle of the river,
where there's never a mirror,
to drift, oars up.

My Cousin, the Blue-Tailed Skink

We share so little, cousin,
and certainly not my cruelty,
having accidentally
shut my door upon your tail

and clipped the blue, wriggly bit
right off. Sure, you'll live
like that for however long,
art-less, without the prosthetic

I call loveliness. Cousin,
what do you think of this
scuttling after,
how empathy

contradicts biology?
You, who would have me in a gulp.

Funny Poems

I am trying to trust comedy, but it's not enough,
it's not intrinsically beautiful, it's not always
performed out of love. Whom does it heal,
how does it redeem? Funny
matters, and it means, but not
when merely an excuse. It's more, I suspect,

like slamming a closet door
as soon as I catch sight of myself
in the full-length mirror.
There, *bam*. There, *bam*, There, *bam*.
I'm seven, or maybe six—
there, *bam*—

and then my terrifying uncle
arrives and bellows,
WHAT ARE YOU DOING
TO THAT DOOR?
and pinches me from the room.

I had, of course, already
tied together all of his shoes,
a dozen pairs knotted in the closet
in a dense clump, like some weird meteoroid.
The funny part was done:

I hid under the front porch the rest of the day,
with the mealybugs, the rusty nails, the slimy somethings,
the rank smells in the dank dark,
kept company by his epileptic dog, Blue.

Springtime in Tampa

In the appalling collage over my bed
at the Sheraton Hotel in Tampa, Florida,
a giant seashell has been pasted
onto a cardboard sea, a perfect scallop

that seems happy
because pretty things are happy.

Someone figured out that I like seashells,
and that's true, I like seashells,
and shrimp scampi,
and I'm a Capricorn,

and I like feeling safe
in the sameness of a hotel.

In my hotel room, it's always
day, and then it's always night,
and then Housekeeping comes in again
on the morning tide.

I wish you were here:
hotel sex is the best.

Instead, alone in my room,
I get naked once the luggage arrives,
naked to unpack, to order fish tacos,
to call my octogenarian dad,

to email my detestable old friend
who refuses to be happy.
I get naked to see the city from on high:
I put on my invisible suit made of love,

and in your honor I do
naked jumping jacks on the balcony.

In Dog Years

He was ninety,
almost thirteen in dog years,

the father she watched
on his knees in her sun room,
teasing her Westies too hard.

To start, he'd hold the Get-a-Ball
overhead, let them see;
then he'd hide the toy

behind his back,
and Ace and Misty would jump on him and bark.
He would laugh, flash the ball:

the dogs would leap and twist,
not knowing where the toy had gone.

She dried another dinner plate.

He had played like this
for years, keeping
love from everyone.

Love Song from Malta

Where are you? The world's askew:
emotions in motion in bodies at rest.
Here in Malta, atop Fort Elmo,
even the ragged pennants can't decide

which wind they're in: a feral cat hisses at
a shimmer in her saucer,
and a pink tourist family huffs to the top
of the battlements, finally,

only to bicker over who holds the map.
By the War Memorial, green buses growl,
guttural with diesel,
patient with need.

On parade, half-naked teens
preen for a selfie—
until a shy girl panics,
musses a cutie's Mohawk, and all the girls

squeal to safety down Triq ir-Reppublika
and into the McDonald's bathroom.
(The pink tourist family hydrates, sensibly.)
In the photo the past will be,

the pink tourist family—
pink on the outside, German on the inside—
gasps as the smallest giant son
skims away a new straw hat,

beyond understanding, to the tide below.
Oh, the hat like a slow gull . . .
White caps. Pink mouths open. *Ach*.
But I see what the kid was hoping for,

the pleasure unplanned.
The Sliema ferry nears the terminal
and booms and rattles in the slaps of the sea,
down where the cruise ships sell fun.

What do I know? To the traveler,
all the world's a coincidence.
Here is a palace
and palace steps meant for climbing

on a day meant for searing in the sun,
with new joys in new words
to heave-ho home. And later comes
that silly marble, same old moon.

I say dash the planets,
I say throw in the stars.
Fling away every straw hat,
and meet me in Malta.

Lights Out in the Chinese Restaurant

I have found mercy in the world.
I have worn the wrong jacket in cold rain,
an inconvenience I learned
only feels like suffering.

When the lights went out
I had just dried off at last, what a downpour,
and I had a beautiful bite of
salt-and-pepper squid with hot mustard
ready mid-air—
I was finally warm again
in the all-day smells of the steamy restaurant,

as a famous ingénue at a corner table
snuffled her lover's ear.
You know her, she was in
that film, oh, you know.
If she had seen me, she would have smiled.

In the booth to my left, a guy in a gray suit
was shouting into his cell,
HE HONESTLY DOESN'T THINK
HE HAS A PROBLEM.

Lights out, and there I was
dead, spinning on the lazy Susan
with the dead, splashed in a bowl,
hot tea poured on me, I was scrubbed,
my eyes were chilies,
the blade was sure, I was a dead pig,
I was boxed, I was mid-air,
I was a bite of salt-and-pepper squid,
I was eaten, I ate me.

Then the lights came back on
and we blinked around,
surprised to see one another.
Nothing had happened,
and everything was true.

I had to shout to be heard,
and here I go again:
IT'S OKAY!
NOTHING HAPPENS AND EVERYTHING IS TRUE.

Night Swim

Without the moon, everyone's a realist.
Along the far cove,
too many strokes from here,
the forms of trees
are trees, the only world.

But if a man
is lucky
and doesn't panic in the middle of his life,
he can swim
until the moon slides over,
bathes him
all in metaphor.

Until the water
reaches,
thins to muck, steps to shore,

and the swimmer stands,
toweling off, trudging back
up the mean hill to the little hotel.

That's the body: a little hotel.
Pay up, says the cold shiver.

Royalty

I always wanted to be the guy pumping gas,
the guy with the white glove opening the door,
letting the kid press the button for the fifth floor,

the guy with the towel over his wrist, pouring,
the guy taking the donation on the phone,
waving to the folks back home.

The guy who could be an intermediary,
who could make my grandfather a king.
My grandfather was never a king, not even in Brooklyn.

But he was carried to his grave, in Brooklyn.
In my best suit, I put my shoulder to him.

O Muse, Recount to Me the Causes

It's not as though the world is all that marvelous,

Or the next world will be either,

With its beetles
Ferrying us,
And all of that mold everywhere,
And each terror we imagine,

Or the world after that,
How can I talk about the world after that,
With the bombs?

It's only a painting,
God tells us,
On the wall of the house of prayer.

And that's not even a colorful sunset—
It's unworthy of our clichés.

Will it matter that the light
Catches a feeling in me?
Feelings are what everybody has.
No one asked to share
The garnet interior of my joy.

I have found that sitting on a park bench
At the brink of humanity
Has made me tired
Of sitting on a park bench
Watching everyone,
Which is what eternity must be like.

If I could, I would stop pretending
Being emptied
Without cease,
And again tomorrow,
Will water any ground, or make anything grow.

In this soil?
Armed only
With a trowel and a couple of words?

Three Possibilities

1.
To come back to life as another man,
but made of love.

To pack a sandwich and a bag of cherries,
to get on the bus at the first stop,
slide sideways, step to the back,

and wave as we go by
to a boy as he fishes in the River of Time.

Then to ride the bus to the terminus,
the morning light flashing between
badly remembered dreams,
forehead pressed to the cold glass.

2.
Or to return as a locust tree's
smooth seed
kept in the pocket of a boy's favorite jeans.

The boy stands on the bank
of the river, and fishes—
and for his lunch
a sandwich and a bag of cherries.

To be the seed rubbed between
thumb and forefinger,
the sure seed,
made of love, the lucky seed.

3.

Or to return as a single sweet cherry,
bountiful, as I have not been,

whole, as I have not been,
red and rich and round,
as I have not been,

good, as I have not been,
made of love, as I have not been,
with a moon inside, a secret.

Neither to be lost between
possibilities,
nor to be swept along

in the River of Time,
where I am, what I have been.

A Little Chat I'll Have with the Very Next Horse I Meet

Please, Master, teach me
to shuck the wrong blanket,
spurn the wrong touch,
to turn so surely with others,
and not to plod, and not to dunder,
but to be better at being awake.

Look, the clouds are scampering together
like cousins after dinner—how do you
keep so still as the light stampedes
over the hill and over the two far trees,
and you, all horse, in the nothingness?
Teach me to shudder off what bites me, Master.
Teach me to welcome someone home.

Not to trust—and then to trust.
Not to run. To run. Oh, to run.
To stand for handling,
to let myself be loved.

To be bigger than I am.
To arch and stretch
and bite the fruit over the fence—
death scares me, Master.

To praise the air with form.
To go where my legs will go.
There's a balance to the body—
Master, will you share?
To step across the meadow,
to trot through the gulley,
to prance on my fingertips and toes.

Notes

The epigraph from Giacomo Puccini's opera *La Bohème* (1896) is sung by Rudolfo Mimi in act 1; the title of the aria, "Che gelida manina," translates literally as "what a gelatinous little hand."

"Enough" is for Beatrice Danzig.

"A Partial List of Our Demands" is after a poem by the Maltese poet Amelie Josephus.

"The Dog Misses You": With growing appreciation for https://translate.google.com.

"On Not Burning a Matisse": Henri Matisse's "The Nightmare of the White Elephant" (color stencil print, 1947) may be found in his *Jazz* portfolio. Owned by the Philadelphia Museum of Art, the work is not on display. The poem takes up the story of Olga Dogaru, a Romanian woman who claimed to have burned seven masterpieces stolen by her son from Rotterdam's Kunsthall Gallery in 2012.

"The Use of the Second Person" is after Spike Lee's film, *Do the Right Thing* (1989).

"Another Bug": The quotation from Hilde Meiner may be found in *Phantasms of Selfhood* (Coric Editions, 1987). The poem features a cameo by the Greek philosopher Epictetus, c. 55–135.

"The Serengeti": "The bewilderments of the eyes are of two kinds, and arise from two causes, either from coming out of the light or from going into the light." Socrates to Glaucon, *The Republic of Plato* (Vintage Classics, 1991), translation by Benjamin Jowett.

"Postcard from Spain" borrows its title from a poem by Langston Hughes.

"A Poppy Seed" is for Czesław Miłosz.

"Let's Go: Arkansas" is after Adam Zagajewski's "To Go to Lvov" and features a cameo by the writer Mark Barr.

"Reading *Antony and Cleopatra* at the Airport Again": The quotation is from Shakespeare's *Antony and Cleopatra*, 4.5.41–42.

"Ein Künstlerroman": A Künstlerroman is a subtype of the German novel genre known as Bildungsroman, which "has as its main theme the formative years or spiritual education of one person" (*Oxford English Dictionary*). A Künstlerroman describes the education of, specifically, an artist.

"Letter to the Grand High Commissioner of the Maltese Police Marching Band" is for Darren and Rosanne Tanti.

"Letter to the Buddha, Including an X-ray of My Foot" is for Christine Marshall.

"Candying Mint": The quotation from Martin Buber may be found in his 1911 essay "The Renewal of Judaism," in *The Martin Buber Reader* (Palgrave, 2002), translation by Walter Kaufmann. Melissa Clark's recipe for candying mint first appeared in 2007 in *Bon Appétit*.

"Love Song from Malta" borrows the phrase "the pleasure unplanned" from the early twentieth-century writings of the French mystic Marie Bamarque, in *Visions and Scenes* (Teal Press, 1983), translated by René Drouin.

"Lights Out in the Chinese Restaurant" features a cameo by the actor Catherine Keener.

"O Muse, Recount to Me the Causes" is after a poem by Hafez. The poem's title borrows from Virgil's *Aeneid*, 1:8, "Musa, mihi memora causa . . ." (translation mine).

"A Little Chat I'll Have with the Very Next Horse I Meet" is for Katherine Min.

Acknowledgments

Thank you to the following journals, and their kind editors, for publication of earlier versions of the poems:

American Poetry Review: "A Little Chat I'll Have with the Very Next Horse I Meet," "Ein Künstlerroman," "Funny Poems," "I'm Here to Give a Little Talk on Singing," and "Springtime in Tampa"

Birmingham Poetry Review: "The Serengeti"

The Carolina Quarterly: "Candying Mint"

Columbia Poetry Review: "Fetch" and "The Sweetness of the Nectarine"

Copper Nickel: "The Last Page"

Hinchas de Poesia: "My Cousin, the Blue-Tailed Skink"

Island (Tasmania): "The Artist and His Model" and "Royalty"

Moon City Review: "Letter to the Buddha, Including an X-ray of My Foot"

The New Republic: "A Late September Afternoon in the Office of the Birches"

The Pinch: "Enough"

Slate: "After Love"

Smartish Pace: "Postcard from Spain"

Southern Indiana Review: "Let's Go: Arkansas" and "On Not Burning a Matisse"

storySouth: "The Ladder" and "Lights Out in the Chinese Restaurant"

Subtropics: "A Poem for Sally"

The Sun: "The Dog Misses You"

Tikkun: "Influenza Ode (From a Very Tall Building)"

Tuesday: An Art Project: "Three Possibilities"

Waccamaw: "Roadkill"

The Yale Review: "Reading *Antony and Cleopatra* at the Airport Again"

"Candying Mint" appeared in *Best American Poetry 2015*, edited by Sherman Alexie and David Lehman (Scribners, 2015).

"Postcard from Spain" was featured on Poetry Daily, www.poems. com.

"A Late September Afternoon in the Office of the Birches" was a September 2014 selection for Poetry in Plain Sight, a public art project in the city of Winston-Salem, North Carolina.

"The Ladder" was awarded the 2013 Randall Jarrell Poetry Prize by the North Carolina Writers Network.

"Lights Out in the Chinese Restaurant" was awarded the 2014 Randall Jarrell Poetry Prize by the North Carolina Writers Network.

"Postcard from Spain" was awarded second place in the 2013 Erskine J. Poetry Competition by *Smartish Pace*.

"Let's Go: Arkansas" and "On Not Burning a Matisse" were finalists for the 2014 Mary C. Mohr Award from the *Southern Indiana Review*.

To the Corporation of Yaddo; the Office of the President, Davidson College; Lena and Dominic at il-Kapitali (Malta); the St. James Cavalier Centre for Creativity (Malta); and the Virginia Center for the Creative Arts, thank you for the support. I am grateful to Jeffrey Levine, Jim Schley, and Marie Gauthier at Tupelo Press, *mille grazie*, and grateful for the gifts of Bronwyn Becker. With thanks as well to those who were made to read half-fledged versions of some of these poems along the way, and then offered advice so clearly right even I had to agree eventually: James Baldacchino, Tony Barnstone, Bruce Cohen, Henri Cole, Cynthia Hogue, Jameelah Lang, Corey Marks, Kevin Prufer, and always, Felicia van Bork.

Other Books from Tupelo Press

Fasting for Ramadan: Notes from a Spiritual Practice (memoir),
  Kazim Ali

Another English: Anglophone Poems from Around the World (anthology),
  edited by Catherine Barnett and Tiphanie Yanique

Pulp Sonnets (poems, with drawings by Amin Mansouri),
  Tony Barnstone

Brownwood (poems), Lawrence Bridges

Everything That Is Broken Up Dances (poems), James Byrne

One Hundred Hungers (poems), Lauren Camp

New Cathay: Contemporary Chinese Poetry (anthology),
  edited by Ming Di

Calazaza's Delicious Dereliction (poems), Suzanne Dracius,
  translated by Nancy Naomi Carlson

Gossip and Metaphysics: Russian Modernist Poetry and Prose (anthology),
  edited by Katie Farris, Ilya Kaminsky, and Valzhyna Mort

Poverty Creek Journal (lyric memoir), Thomas Gardner

The Good Dark (poems), Annie Guthrie

My Immaculate Assassin (novel), David Huddle

Halve (poems), Kristina Jipson

Dancing in Odessa (poems), Ilya Kaminsky

A God in the House: Poets Talk About Faith (interviews),
  edited by Ilya Kaminsky and Katherine Towler

Third Voice (poems), Ruth Ellen Kocher

Cooking with the Muse (cookbook and poetry anthology), Myra Kornfeld
  and Stephen Massimilla

Boat (poems), Christopher Merrill

A Camouflage of Specimens and Garments (poems), Jennifer Militello

Canto General: Song of the Americas (poems), Pablo Neruda, translated by
  Mariela Griffor

Lucky Fish (poems), Aimee Nezhukumatathil

Ex-Voto (poems), Adélia Prado, translated by Ellen Doré Watson

Mistaking Each Other for Ghosts (poems), Lawrence Raab

Intimate: An American Family Photo Album (hybrid memoir),
  Paisley Rekdal

Vivarium (poems), Natasha Sajé

Wintering (poems), Megan Snyder-Camp

Swallowing the Sea (essays), Lee Upton

Butch Geography (poems), Stacey Waite

SEE OUR COMPLETE LIST AT WWW.TUPELOPRESS.ORG